by Geoff Preston

in easy steps and **in easy steps pocket** are imprints of
Computer Step
Southfield Road . Southam . Warwickshire CV47 OFB . England
Website: www.ineasysteps.com
Email: books@ineasysteps.com

Notice of Liability
Every effort has been made to ensure that this book contains
accurate and current information. However, Computer Step and
the author shall not be liable for any loss or damage suffered by
readers as a result of any information contained herein.

Trademarks
All trademarks are acknowledged as belonging to their
respective companies.

Printed and bound in the United Kingdom

ISBN 1-84078-164-5

My Mobile Phone

Warning: Don't let anyone else see your PIN

Phone Number

Make

Model

Date Purchased

Serial Number *(Make a note of the serial no. If the phone's lost or stolen, the police may ask for it.)*

PIN *(Always use a PIN. When you switch on, you will need to enter your PIN to activate the phone. A great security device, but don't forget it.)*

PUK Code *(If your phone is blocked, call your service provider and ask for the PUK unblocking code.)*

Operator *(BT Cellnet, One2One, Orange, Virgin, Vodafone, etc)*

Service Provider *(The company to whom you pay the bill)*

Emergency Number *(To report a lost or stolen phone)*

Special thanks to Simon and Sally who did a great deal of research for me and provided lots of help and advice. And the occasional use of their phones.

Contents

2. Text Messaging

1

Introduction

When Alexander Graham Bell invented the telephone in 1876, he couldn't have imagined how it would change our lives. Within a few decades the phone was commonplace in homes in England. A few decades later, phones were in common use throughout most of the northern hemisphere. By the mid 1960s people in England could telephone people in America or Australia and hold a conversation almost as though they were standing next to each other.

But, if you didn't have a phone in your home or you wanted to make a call whilst away from home, the *only* option at that time was to use a public call box.

The biggest development in telephony since Bell's invention is undoubtedly the mobile, or cellular phone.

Not long ago, the only way to make a phone call away from home was using a public phone box. The advent of mobile phones has led to a gradual decline in their numbers, and an increase in vandalism has led to a change in their design. Where in the UK can you find phone boxes painted cream? The answer is on page 116.

Dr Martin Cooper –
the father of the cellular phone

Mobile phones have been around for a surprisingly long time. But early versions were very heavy largely due to the huge batteries that had to be carried around to provide them with enough power to send and receive signals.

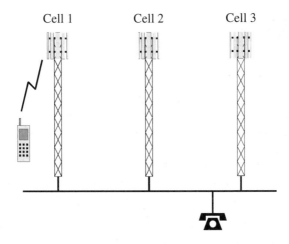

Cell 1   Cell 2   Cell 3

Each cell has its own station which can transmit to, and receive signals from, cellular phones. The base stations are connected to the existing telephone network. A mobile phone automatically communicates with the nearest base station, and the call is either routed to a land telephone or to the base station nearest to the cellular phone of the person receiving the call.

DID YOU KNOW

The first call made on a cellular phone was by its inventor, Dr Martin Cooper. He called his rival, Joel Engel, Head of Research at Bell Laboratories to tell him that he'd succeeded in inventing a working cellular phone!

DID YOU KNOW

Some mobile phones can display cell information so you can tell which cell you are using.

The breakthrough came in 1973 when Dr Martin Cooper of Motorola proposed a cellular phone system. The idea was that the country would be divided into areas or cells, each with its own base station.

Mobile phone masts are now a common site on tall buildings. The long vertical slats send and receive signals from mobile phones. Many masts serve more than one operator.

Some people are concerned that the emissions from the receivers may be harmful. There has been a great deal of debate about whether they should be placed near schools or on private dwellings.

In urban areas cellular masts are erected on tall buildings, but in the countryside they often have to be mounted on their own tower. These are criticised because they spoil the countryside. But we have to make a decision: do we want cellular phones? If we do, then this is the price we have to pay.

This picture shows a tower in St Albans, Hertfordshire which is being extended to provide better coverage. The men are working on a One2One extension at the top of the tower. The lower gallery is for Vodafone.

Masts like these can be seen all across the country. Are they any more unsightly than electricity pylons?

In an attempt to satisfy environmentalists who criticised phone companies for erecting unsightly masts, one company took the unusual step of trying to disguise the mast as a tree. However, masts have to be sited away from obstructions like other trees as they obstruct the signals, so they tend to look a bit odd on their own.

It's hard to imagine what it must have been like for users of early cellphones which were large and very heavy. Microelectronics has meant that phones have become smaller and lighter. Battery technology has also contributed to the lightness and practicality of modern phones. Imagine a phone that takes more than a working day to recharge, yet provides only half-an-hour's use? Compare these two, which are just over a quarter of a century apart.

The First Cellphone (1973)
        Make/Model : Motorola Dyna-Tac
        Size : 230 x 51 x 45 mm
        Weight : 1.1 kilos
        Display : None
        Talk time : 35 minutes
        Recharge time : 10 hours
        Additional features : None

The Latest Cellphone (2002)
        Make/Model : Nokia 6210
        Size : 130 x 47 x 19 mm
        Weight : 114 gms
        Display : LCD (7 lines of text)
        Talk time : 270 minutes
        Recharge time : 1 hour
        Additional features : WAP, data, text

Having Fun

A modern mobile phone is more than just a means of talking to your friends while you're standing in a field. Today's cellular phone is a diary, a notebook, a watch, a means of sending notes, an amusement arcade and much, much more.

In this book I hope to be able to show you some of the interesting things you can do with your mobile phone, but first some words of caution.

Caring for your Phone

It's easy to think that because your phone was free, or nearly free, it can be replaced for free. In almost all cases, the cost of the phone was subsidised by the service provider. In other words, you pay a slightly higher price for calls which repays the phone company for initially giving you the phone at a greatly reduced price. If you lose or break your phone, you'll get a shock when you find out the cost of a replacement. So you need to look after it.

DID YOU
KNOW

The cost of a mobile phone is likely to be far more than you paid for it.

Insurance

It may be worth considering insurance for your phone. You may be able to include it on your household insurance, or alternatively your phone supplier should be able to recommend a good insurance policy to cover the phone for the full replacement cost if lost or stolen.

High Theft Risk

Mobile phones are small, lightweight and highly desirable. Therefore they are a high priority target for thieves.

- Record the serial number of the phone so that if it does get stolen, you can give the number to the police.

- Do not carry your phone on your belt where everyone can see it. It looks good, but it's an open invitation to thieves.

- Don't take your phone out unless you know you're going to need it. Just like carrying around large sums of money, it's a pain having to constantly monitor it.

- Don't leave your phone lying around unattended. If a phone is unattended, it's surprising how quickly it grows legs and walks away.

Don't lend your phone to anyone, not even your best friend. If they lose it or run up a large bill, you may find you're not friends much longer.

If your phone is lost or stolen, report it to your service provider immediately and then to the police if you're sure it has been stolen. Your service provider will be able to block the phone so it can't be used and in the case of 'Pay As You Go' phones, any credit can normally be transferred to a new phone. If you have insurance on your phone and it has been stolen, your insurers will want a crime reference number which you get from the police when you report its theft.

Using your Phone

Hundreds of mobile phones are handed in to police and transport staff every year. Many are never reunited with their owners. But many could be returned if owners took the trouble to place a sticker on the inside of the phone showing their name and postcode. You don't have to spoil the look of the phone: you can fix a label inside where it isn't normally seen. If possible, use a pen which only shows up under ultraviolet light.

COOL
TIP

Don't write your name and postcode on the fascia or battery which can easily be replaced.

PIN and PUK

You can prevent unauthorised use of your phone and hence prevent a large phone bill if your phone is lost or stolen. The method is simple – use a Personal Identification Number or PIN. Most phones can be set so that when they're switched on a secret code has to be entered before they will work.

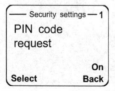

The PIN is usually a four-digit code and should be something that's easy for you to remember, but not so obvious that anyone can work it out.

If several unsuccessful attempts to enter the PIN have been made, some phones may display a message saying that they are blocked. If this happens you'll need to enter a PUK code and the phone cannot be used until the code has been entered.

The Personal Unblocking Key (PUK) code can only be obtained from your service provider. Many service providers now have an automated service for giving out the PUK code, but you will have to enter some details including, possibly, account details.

Inconsiderate use

Mobile phones are not everyone's first love. For many they are a source of constant annoyance and their use at certain times can at best be described as inconsiderate.

WATCH
OUT

Consider those around you before using your phone. Switch your phone off before entering a cinema or theatre.

Apart from the actual conversation, the constant ringing can be an annoyance to those around you.

Many phones are fitted with a vibrating alert which enables you to set your phone to ring, vibrate or both when there is an incoming voice call or text message. This simply means that you feel it ringing rather than everyone else nearby hearing it. If you have a vibrating feature on your phone, select it when you're in an enclosed public space like on a train. If you don't have such a feature, and you really must have the phone on, set the ringtone as quietly as it will go.

COOL
TIP

If your phone has a silent ring feature, use it whenever a ringing phone would be an irritant to others.

Silent alerts

Many phone shops sell flashing aerials which replace the existing aerial.

When the phone rings, the aerial flashes to warn you. It works by detecting the signals that are sent to and from mobile phones. The trouble is that if someone near to you receives a call on their mobile, it might make your aerial flash. You can only have an aerial like this fitted to phones which are themselves fitted with an external aerial.

Like the flashing aerial, the pen below has a special sensor which detects the signals made by a mobile phone. When the phone rings, a light at the top of the pen flashes. This is a lot less irritating than a loud ringing tone.

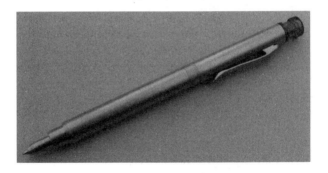

The advantage with the flashing aerial is that it's powered by the phone whereas the pen requires batteries that run down quite quickly.

Vibrating battery

If your phone doesn't have a vibrating alert, you can buy a vibrating battery.

These are a little bulkier than standard batteries, but are an accessory worth having if you don't want to annoy others with your phone constantly ringing.

Safety

There is a theory that mobile phone use may be harmful. Opinion is divided on the subject but if you are in any doubt, why not buy a personal hands-free kit. Most phones can be fitted with a hands-free kit which comprises an earphone (or maybe two if you want to listen in both ears), an inline microphone (which is attached to the same cable as one of the earphones and dangles near your mouth) and an interface to connect to your phone.

COOL
TIP

If you fit a hands-free kit, check to see if your phone will automatically answer an incoming call.

In the Car

Using a mobile phone whilst driving is highly dangerous and could soon become a specific motoring offence. If you really must use your phone in the car, use a hands-free car kit.

A purpose-built and professionally installed hands-free kit can be set up to automatically mute the radio when the phone is in use and can even be installed so that the conversation comes through the car's stereo speakers.

A cheaper alternative is the type that fits into the car's cigarette lighter socket and provides a secure cradle for the phone. This kit can be easily transferred to another car.

On the Desk

It's important to look after your phone wherever it is. Many people take special care of it when it's being carried, but when it's in the home it's frequently left in no particular place. As a result it gets knocked off shelves and often can't be found.

If you have your own desk, buy a desktop cradle and get into the habit of putting your phone into it when you're indoors.

Even better than a simple cradle to hold your phone is a desktop charger. One of the main causes for a mobile not working is that the battery is flat, but if every time the phone is brought into the house it's dropped into its charger, the phone will always be ready for use, and if it rings whilst it's charging you can answer it without getting caught up in the lead from the plug-in charger.

Spare Batteries

If keeping your battery charged is a problem, why not get a second battery?

Large capacity battery

Battery technology, together with more efficient electronics, has meant that batteries have got smaller and smaller, and the time between charges has got greater. But if the talk time and standby time is still not long enough, try a battery with a larger capacity which can add as much as 50% onto your phone's talk time and standby time before it needs recharging.

The drawback is that they are usually a little thicker and heavier than the standard battery.

When buying a new battery, always choose Li-Ion (Lithium Ion) or NiMH (Nickel Metal Hydride). Avoid the cheaper Nickel Cadmium batteries which do not like constant re-charging before they're completely flat.

Care for spare batteries

It is most important to store any spare batteries carefully. If possible, keep your old spare battery in the case in which your new battery was packaged. In particular...

- Don't let anything touch the contacts.

- Do not attempt to take it apart.

- Do not store it in a place where it could get hot.

🔋 Dispose of unwanted batteries according to the instructions printed on the battery or its packaging.

On your Person

Mobile phones get dropped. It's inevitable. I've lost count of the number of times I've put my phone into my shirt pocket, bent down to pick something up and the phone has fallen out.

You usually have to drop a phone a long way and onto a very hard surface to do any serious damage like breaking the screen, but the cover (fascia) of the phone can suffer. If you are prone to dropping your phone you may like to consider a protective case.

More and more phones are equipped with removable fascias. If you get tired of one fascia or your phone is damaged because you dropped it, a new fascia can be bought quite cheaply and fitted in seconds. New fascias can sometimes be fitted to phones that don't have user-replaceable fascias. For these phones you may need a special tool to remove the old fascia and this is really a job for experts as opening such a phone could nullify the warranty.

An alternative to replacing the fascia is to protect it, and there are countless leather phone cases available which offer a degree of padding, so should the unthinkable happen and you drop your phone onto a hard surface, the leather may provide a little extra protection.

Leather carry cases are really designed to protect the phone (in particular the window) from scratches which you pickup from normal, everyday use. The trouble with them is that it you've got a nice fascia, the leather case will cover it up. If you want to show off your fascia, and you want to protect it, try using a clear plastic case.

When carrying your phone around, it looks really cool to clip it onto your belt with the hook that's usually fitted to the back of the leather carry case. Unfortunately what this does is to advertise to the world that you have a mobile phone and an opportunist thief wouldn't think twice about trying to steal it – possibly injuring the owner whilst trying to wrench it off their belt.

 Keep your phone out of sight.

WATCH
OUT

Keep your phone in your inside pocket or in your bag so that it's out of sight. Obviously when you want to use your phone you've got to take it out, but at all other times keep it hidden.

Accessories

There is a whole new industry built up around mobile phones. Having a phone is great, but there are countless accessories available to add to the fun. Here are just two of my favourites...

Joystick for Snake

For several years phone manufacturers have been using up the surplus memory in phones to include games to amuse yourself when life becomes quiet. Of all the games on all the phones, Nokia's Snake (and the later Snake II) has proved most popular.

But the phone's keypad is the drawback. Not only is the keypad less than satisfactory for entering text messages, it's also not best suited to playing games. To overcome this, one company has produced a little joystick that clips onto the front of your phone enabling you to control the snake a lot better.

Hologram

A hologram is a 3D picture. When viewed at slightly different angles you get the impression of 'depth' and objects in the hologram appear to be three-dimensional.

Holograms are now very cheap, and small, transparent, self-adhesive ones can be fitted onto your phone's screen. Because they're transparent you can still see the screen through the hologram.

There are several Internet companies selling phone accessories including MobileFun at *http://mobilefun.co.uk/*

Using your Phone Abroad

Running a mobile phone in the UK can be quite expensive. Service charges or line rental, added to the relatively high cost of calls and text messages can create quite a bill. That cost is, of course, after you've bought the phone.

But all of this can pale into insignificance when compared to the cost of taking your mobile phone overseas.

In addition to the cost of the calls you make which is paid to your operator, you may also be charged for the air time belonging to the service provider in the country in which you are using the phone. You're not paying twice for the call, but you will have to paying your operator for the UK part of the call and also the foreign operator for the foreign part of the call. As if that isn't bad enough, you may also have to pay the operator in the country you are staying in for calls made *to* your phone.

WATCH OUT

It's very easy to run up a 3-figure phone bill whilst you're away for a fortnight's holiday in a European country like Spain.

But, if you really feel a phone is essential (and for emergencies, it probably is worth taking a phone abroad) then you must do several things before you leave…

1. Contact your service provider to find out if your phone will work in the country to which you are travelling.

2. If it will work, you may need to ask your service provider if there is a bar on overseas use, and if so, if it can be lifted.

3. If you've got through the first two steps, find out if your operator has an arrangement with a service provider in the foreign country you are visiting. If they have, find out the name.

4. Although not essential, it's worth finding out the number that must be dialled to access your voicemail. Dialling from overseas may require a different number. You may also need to enter a security code after dialling the number. Find out exactly what you have to do.

COOL
TIP

If you do get an overseas bar lifted, you may find it will be blocked after you return. Check whether the bar is lifted before each visit overseas.

5. Check all numbers in your phone are in the international format. You should replace the '0' at the start of a number and replace it with '+44'. Therefore the number...

020 7123 4567

becomes...

+44 20 7123 4567

COOL TIP

Always put a PIN number on your phone and keep it switched off while you are on holiday. That way, if it is lost or stolen, the 'finder' can't run up a huge bill that you could be asked to pay.

Finally, check with your household insurance to see if your phone is covered for loss or theft whilst it is out of the country.

Overseas use

If your UK operator (BT Cellnet, One2One, Orange, Vodafone or Virgin) recommends a particular overseas operator, when you arrive at your holiday destination check your phone is connected to it. Normally, the choice of network connection is automatically selected by the phone, but you can override this and select a network manually, hence ensuring that you use the service which offers the best deal financially and, in some cases, the best reception.

| Go through the menus on your phone to find **Network selection**.

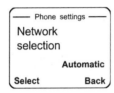

2 Choose **Manual**. The phone will then scan for all available networks.

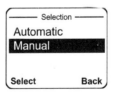

3 Choose the operator you require. When in France, for example, you may find you have a choice between SFR and Itineris, whilst in Spain you will see something like AirTel, Amena and Movistar.

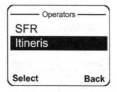

LEARN BY
HEART

When you return to the UK, change the Network selection back to Automatic.

2

Text Messaging

One of the fastest growing uses of mobiles phones is not speaking and listening, but sending text messages. The ability to send messages as text was seen almost as a gimmick when it was introduced in the mid 1990s.

DID YOU KNOW

The Philippines is the text messaging capital of the world, with more than 32 million text messages passing through the networks each day.

In the early days of text messaging it was only possible to send messages to phones on the same network. So, if you were connected to the Vodafone network, you could only send messages to friends who were also on the Vodafone network. If a particular friend was on Orange, Cellnet or One2One, then you'd have to find another way of contacting them. In 1999 that changed and it became possible to send a text message to other mobile phones regardless of whether or not the receiving phone was on the same network as the sender's phone.

In May 2000, 1 billion text messages were sent by the Germans when the total volume for Europe for that month was 4 billion.

Text messaging is known as SMS – Short Message Service. The important word here is 'short'. Each text message may be a maximum of 160 characters in length if you use the Latin alphabet. For non-Latin alphabets such as Arabic and Chinese, the limit is 70 characters.

The first text message is said to have been sent in December 1992 from a PC to a mobile phone on the Vodafone GSM network in the United Kingdom.

The popularity of SMS is largely due to the fact that it's cheaper to text than to speak. But its popularity with phone companies is because it is seen as an invitation to make a voice call which generates more revenue.

The main restriction with short messages is that they are short. But a long message service is planned.

Why use SMS?

Sending text messages is fun for both the sender and for the person receiving them, but it is often more convenient than making a phone call. Here are some other reasons to use text...

ф   Sending and receiving text doesn't disturb anyone else, so use text if you're in a public place or in a quiet place. *(Loud rings and even louder conversations can be annoying, especially when those around can only hear one half of the conversation!)*

ф   Even if the receiving phone is switched off, the message will get through to the person when the phone is switched on again. *(A voice call requires the person to be at the other end of the phone. You can leave a message on their voicemail, but they will have to pay to retrieve it.)*

Text is much cheaper than making a voice call. *(The current cost of sending a text message is about 10p per message plus VAT. A voice call can be as much as 35p per minute. In most cases, text message retrieval is free. The exception is if you pay to receive messages like news updates.)*

It's great if you want to give information like an email address which could easily be copied wrongly if it's spoken. *(Dictating an email address or an Internet URL is difficult and subject to errors. You only need one error in an email address to ensure it won't work. Sending it by SMS is much more reliable.)*

How to Send Text

All phones are slightly different, so you may have to look at the manual for your particular phone to see exactly how you should do it.

Setup

You may first have to set up your phone so that you can send and receive text messages.

| Press the **Menu** button.

2 Choose **Message settings**. This may be in the **Messages** menu, or in the **Settings** menu.

3 Choose **Message centre number** for your network. This should be...

Cellnet	+44780 200 0332
One2One	+44795 887 9879
Orange	+44797 310 0973
Virgin	+44795 887 9989
Vodafone	+44778 501 6005

LEARN BY HEART

Enter the number in its international format. (Remove the leading '0' and replace it with +44)

4   Choose **Messages sent as** and select **Text**.

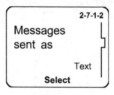

```
                                    2-7-1-2
      Messages
      sent as

                          Text
               Select
```

5   (Optional) Choose **Message validity** and select **Maximum**.

6   (Optional) Choose **Delivery reports**. If you want to receive a report telling you that a message has been received, select **Yes**, otherwise select **No**.

Sending a message

1   Press the **Menu** button.

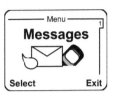

2   Choose **Messages** or **Messaging**.

3   Choose **Send message** or **Write message**.

4   Enter the text of your message.

5   Choose **Send**. (You may have to choose **Options** first, and then **Send**.)

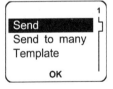

6   Enter the phone number of the person you are sending the message to and press **Send**.

Entering the text

Each key on the phone can enter more than one character. For example, the number 5 key can also enter the letters J, K or L. To enter L, press the 5 key three times (quickly). You'll see the character entered on the screen begins as J, changes to K and then to L. So, to type the word LOVE, you would press key 5 three times, key 6 three times, key 8 three times and key 3 twice. The space is usually entered by pressing 0 (zero, not the letter 'O') and the full stop is usually key 1.

The Problems with Texting

There are two problems with text messaging. The first is that you are limited to 160 characters. This means your message is going to have to be brief (although, with care, it's surprising how much you can get into 160 characters). The second problem is that the phone keypad was designed to enter numbers, not words. As you can see from the example above, entering a message can mean a great deal of key pressing. But, where there's a will, there's a way. Both of these problems can be overcome in more than one way.

LEARN BY HEART

A character is any letter, number or punctuation mark. A space also counts as one character. (How many characters in this tip including the text in brackets? The answer is on page 116.)

Language

Text messaging has generated its own special language partly due to the need to keep messages within the 160 character limit, but also to try to reduce the number of key presses. (To enter the word 'LOVE' requires 11 key presses.)

TLAs

Although these existed long before text messaging came to be, Three Letter Acronyms, or TLAs as they have become known, allow the user to enter a group of three letters to represent a phrase. The subheading above is in itself a Three Letter Acronym and regular texters seeing the letters TLA would immediately know what it meant.

DID YOU
KNOW

There are 17,576 (26x26x26) combinations of TLAs starting with AAA and ending with ZZZ.

   Some of the huge number of TLAs are not really useful for the average text message so I've just included some that I think are most likely to be useful (or that I think are funny or clever).

COOL
TIP

To avoid others knowing you're receiving text messages, set the phone to vibrate rather than ring when a message arrives. To avoid annoying others whilst sending a text message, switch off the keytones (the beep when a key is pressed).

A

AAB	above and beyond
AAN	an amazing night
AAO	all at once
AFK	away from keyboard
AFN	all for nothing
AIQ	all is quiet
AKA	also known as
AMM	and much more
AMQ	another moronic (or meaningless) question
AOB	any other business
AOK	all okay (alright)
APB	all points bulletin
AUB	are you bored?
AYA	and yet again

B

BAB	bring a bottle
BBQ	barbecue
BBS	bulletin board system
BBT	big bang theory

BEM	bug-eyed monster
BFF	best friends forever
BFG	big friendly giant
BFN	bye for now
BLT	bacon, lettuce and tomato
BNB	bed and breakfast
BOF	boring old fart
BRB	be right back
BTL	better than life
BTW	by the way
BYO	bring your own

C

CDS	compact disc single
COA	change of address

D

DWH	don't walk here
DZB	dozy bugger

E

EAE	each and every
EBT	every bloody time
EFT	electronic funds transfer
EOD	every other day/end of day
EOE	end of everything/ errors and omissions excepted
EOL	end of line

EOM	end of message
EOR	either/or
EOW	end of week
ESP	extra-sensory perception
ETA	estimated time of arrival
ETD	estimated time of departure
EZJ	easy job

F

FAO	for the attention of
FAQ	frequently asked questions
FHS	for heaven's sake
FOC	free of charge
FYA	for your attention
FYC	for your consideration
FYI	for your information
FYJ	for your journal

G

GAY	good as you
GFK	go fly a kite
GTG	got to go
GTH	go to hell

H

HAK	hugs and kisses
HTH	hope this helps
HYP	hypertension

I

IAC	in any case
IAE	in any event
IAW	in another world
ICQ	I seek you
IFL	in a former life
IIC	if I'm correct
IIF	if I fail
IIR	if I recall/if I remember
IOW	in other words
ITY	I thank you
IUA	if you accept
IUC	if you can
IUW	if you want
IWH	I was here
IWU	I want you

J

JBC	just because I can
JDI	just do it
JFK	just for kicks
JFL	just for laughs

JFM	just for me
JFU	just for us
JFY	just for you
JIT	just in time
JOJ	just off the jet
JWU	just when you

K

KDF	knocked down flat
KFC	Kentucky Fried Chicken
KOD	knocked out

L

LMG	let me go
LMK	let me know
LOL	laughs out loud
LOS	loss of signal
LUE	life, the universe and everything

M

MCP	male chauvinist pig
MHO	my humble opinion
MIB	men in black
MOR	middle of the road
MUD	multi-user dungeon
MUG	multi-user game

N

NBG	no bloody good
NCD	no can do
NDG	no damn good
NFW	no flipping way
NGA	no good anyway
NMP	not my problem
NMS	not my solution
NOB	no other business
NRN	no reply necessary
NUS	National Union of Students

O

OAO	over and out
OAW	on another world
OIC	oh, I see!
OMO	on my own
ONO	or near offer/or nearest offer
OOT	out of town
OTB	on the ball
OTH	over the hill
OTO	one time only
OTT	over the top
OYO	on your own

P

PDA	personal digital assistant
PDH	pretty damn high
PDQ	pretty damn quick
PIG	pretty intelligent girl
PIN	personal identification number
PIQ	person in question
PMS	pre-menstrual syndrome
PMT	pre-menstrual tension
POE	point of entry
POI	point of information
POV	point of view
PYO	pick your own
PYT	pretty young thing

Q

QOL	quality of life
QWA	quit while (you are) ahead

R

RBM	read the bloody manual
RFI	request for information
RML	read my lips
ROX	right on target
RQQ	really quick question
RSI	repetitive strain injury
RSN	real soon now

RTI	repetitive talk injury
RTM	read the manual
RTS	ready to send/return to sender
RUS	are you serious?

S

SAF	single Asian female
SAM	single Asian male
SBF	single black female
SBM	single black male
SFK	so far as I know
SWF	single white female
SWM	single white male
SYL	strapping young lad

T

TBA	to be announced/to be arranged
TIA	thanks in advance
TIC	tongue in cheek
TLA	three letter acronym
TLC	tender loving care
TMI	too much information

U

UKM	you kidding me?

V

VIP	very important person
VVE	very very easy
VVH	very very hard

W

WCS	worst case scenario
WGO	what's going on?
WOT	what's on television
WTH	what the hell?

X

XST	extra special thoughts

Y

YAM	yet another mistake
YBS	your big sister
YFF	your friend forever
YIS	why am I so stupid?
YNM	you and me
YNW	you're not welcome
YUS	why are you so stupid?
YVW	you're very welcome

Z

ZIF	zero insertion force

BILs

Bracketed Initial Letters are a quick way to send a feeling or thought. If you're going to use these, learn how to enter < and > really quickly.

<B>	Bored	<K>	Kissing You
<C>	Crying	<L>	Laughing
<D>	Dazed	<O>	Overjoyed
<E>	Elated	<R>	Resting
<F>	Fed Up	<S>	Smiling
<G>	Grinning	<T>	Tired
<H>	Happy	<X>	Kissing
<J>	Joking	<Y>	Yawning

Other Abbreviations

The use of abbreviations will reduce the number of characters in your message (remember there's a limit of 160 characters per message), but can also reduce the number of key presses.

Although there are lots of combinations of three letters, there are lots of common phrases that can't be broken down into a TLA. Texters have developed a language all of their own based on abbreviations. Although similar to TLAs, they may contain more than three letters and also include numbers.

Using numbers instead of letters

The only numbers which can be practically used instead of letters are 1 (*I need NE1*), 2 (*I went 2 the park*), 4 (*I went B4*) and 8 (*You are L8*).

1	NE1, SUM1, NO1
2	to, too, 2DAY, 2MORRO, WAN2
4	for, B4, A4D, 4EVR
8	B8, D8, F8, FR8, GR8, H8, IR8, K8, L8, M8, R8, TR8, W8
@	at
#	number

WATCH OUT

Some abbreviations use less characters, but do not require fewer key presses – eg DATE has 4 characters but requires 5 key presses, D8 also requires 5 key presses.

Single letters to represent a word or syllable

Some letters can be used instead of a word or part of a word...

A	Ay?
B	instead of 'be' – B4, BWARE
C	see
D	instead of 'ed' – D8D
N	instead on 'en' – SND, NY
O	instead of 'ow' – GRO, GLO
Q	queue, cue

R	are, instead of 'er' – L8R
T	tea
U	you
X	wrong
Y	why

Abbreviations for single words

Rather than spell out whole words, abbreviate them...

AGD	agreed
APR	April
APX	approximately
AUG	August
AVE	average
BLK	black
BTH	bath
BTM	bottom
BUL	bulletin
CHQ	cheque
DEC	December
DNR	dinner
DZY	dizzy or dozy
ENT	enter or entered
ENV	envelope
ESP	especially
EZ	easy
FEB	February
FLT	flight

FRI	Friday
JAN	January
JUL	July
JUN	June
LUV	love
MAR	March
MAX	maximum
MIN	minimum
MON	Monday
NOV	November
OCT	October
PLS	please
PVT	private
REF	refer to
REP	representative
SAT	Saturday
SEP	September
SUN	Sunday
THX	thanks
TUE	Tuesday
THU	Thursday
TXT	text
USU	usually
WED	Wednesday
WOT	what
WRK	work

| XTC | ecstasy |
| XLNT | excellent |

Initials instead of a phrase

Instead of writing out a whole phrase, you can often abbreviate to the initial letters. Some of these also qualify as TLAs.

AAMOF	as a matter of fact
ASFAIK	as far as I know
ASAP	as soon as possible
ATW	at the weekend
AYNIL	all you need is love
BAS1	be as one
BBFN	bye bye for now
BCNU	be seeing you
BFN	bye for now
BRB	be right back
BTW	by the way
BYKT	but you knew that
CM	call me
CMIIW	correct me if I'm wrong
CUL8R	see you later
CU+CMEST	come up and see me sometime
CU	see you
CU2NITE	see you tonight
CW2CU	can't wait to see you
DK	don't know
DUR?	do you remember

8DAW	eight days a week
EOD	end of discussion
ETYA<3OUT	eat your heart out
F?	friends?
4EVRYRS	forever yours
4YEO	for your eyes only
F2F	face to face
F2T	free to talk
FITB	fill in the blank
FWIW	for what it's worth
FYI	for your information
H2CUS	hope to see you soon
HAK	hugs and kisses
HOT4U	hot for you
HTH	hope this helps
IC	I see
IDK	I don't know
INEZSpsBksRGR8	in easy steps books are great
ITOU	I'm thinking of you
IWHYH	I wanna hold your hand
IMCO	in my considered opinion
IMHO	in my humble opinion
IMNSHO	in my not so humble opinion
IMO	in my opinion
IMW8IN	I'm waiting
IOU	I owe you
IOW	in other words

JBIC	just because I can
J4F	just for fun
KHUF	know how you feel
LMOLM	love me or leave me
LOL	laughing out loud
MGB	may God bless
MHOTY	my hat's off to you
NRN	no reply necessary
OTOH	on the other hand
O4U	only for you
PCM	please call me
ROF	rolling on the floor
ROTFL	rolling on the floor laughing
RSN	real soon now
RUOK?	are you alright?
SITD	still in the dark
SOL	sooner or later
SPK2UL8R	speak to you later
S2US	speak to you soon
SUS	see you soon
SURS	see you really soon
SWAK	sent with a kiss
SWALK	sent with a loving kiss
THNQ	thank you
3SUM	threesome
TIA	thanks in advance
TIC	tongue in cheek

2NITE	tonight
TPTB	the powers that be
TTYL	talk to you later
TYVM	thank you very much
T2ULTR	talk to you later
2D4	to die for
2G4U	too good for you
2L8	too late
2BCTND	to be continued
WAN2	want to
WAN2TLK	want to talk
W4U	waiting for you
1DAFL	wonderful
WUWH	wish you were here
WYSIWYG	what you see is what you get
YPOM?	your place or mine?

WATCH
OUT

Some people frown upon using abbreviations of this type. Be careful how you use them.

Another Way

Predictive text

Abbreviations such as those shown on the previous pages were developed and are used primarily to reduce the number of key presses required to enter simple words. A more sophisticated way is to use Predictive Text. Several phones feature predictive text, but the Nokia system seems particularly effective.

You must first 'switch on' predictive text which means going to the Message settings menu and choosing either Predictive text on or in the case of Nokia phones, choosing Dictionary and selecting a language.

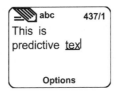

If you're studying French, German or Spanish at school, try selecting one of the foreign language dictionaries and sending messages to your classmates in a foreign language.

COOL
TIP

Entering predictive text is a little confusing at first, but you soon get the hang of it. You only press each key once and the system tries to work out what the word is. Continuing with the example 'LOVE' which I used previously, simply press keys 5, 6, 8 and 3. A line will be drawn under each letter as you type. Each time a letter is pressed, the system will try to make sense of it and in most cases, by the time you get to the end of the word, the system will have worked out what you're trying to write.

Here is an example of how predictive text works (this may differ from one phone to another). When you enter 'LOVE' the first key press will give you <u>K</u>. After the second key press you'll have <u>Ka</u>. At the third key press, the system knows that <u>Kat</u> is not the start of any word it recognises and so it looks at the other possible letters available from the keys you've pressed. At this point the whole word is replaced with <u>Lot</u>. When the fourth key is pressed, the system knows there is no word that begins <u>Lotd</u> and so it looks at other possible combinations of letters. It changes the whole word to <u>Love</u>, which is the word you wanted. Pressing space after the last letter fixes the word.

If you do finish typing and the word you want is not displayed, press the * key to scroll through all the possible alternatives. Entering a space 'fixes' the word, but deleting the space gives you another chance to press * to choose an alternative. For example, if you entered 5, 6, 8 and 3 you will have the word 'LOVE' displayed. However, you may have wanted a different word. You may have wanted 'LOUD'. If you press the * key at this point, the word 'LOUD' is displayed. As you will see from the keys on your phone, 'LOUD' would also be entered with the same four key presses.

LEARN BY HEART

You can use TLAs and abbreviations with predictive text, but you may have to enter all of your abbreviations into the phone's dictionary.

If the word you want is not in the list, if it's a name for example, press Spell and type the word in normally. This will store the word in the dictionary so that if you ever need to type that word again the phone would now be able to recognise it.

Templates

Several phones have a number of Templates stored inside them. The Nokia 6210 carries 10 templates, all but one of which must have something added to them before they can be sent.

The full list of Nokia templates is…

- Please call

- I'm at home. Please call

- I'm at work. Please call

- I'm in a meeting, call me later

- Meeting is cancelled
- I am late. I will be there at
- See you in
- See you at
- Sorry, I can't help you with this.
- I will be arriving at

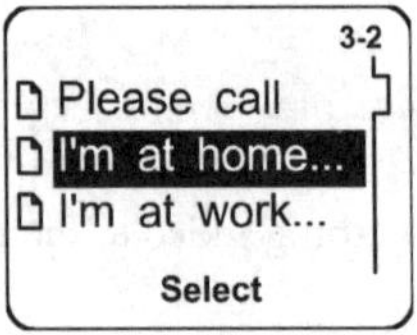

These can be really useful. If you're on a train and you're running late, you can send a message very quickly telling the person who's supposed to be meeting you.

And Yet Another Way

The main drawback with entering text on a phone is that it doesn't have the typewriter style keyboard that we're all used to using to enter text into a computer. There are some alternatives which dedicated texters might like to consider.

The typewriter style keyboard is usually referred to as a QWERTY keyboard after the first 6 letters on the top row of the letter keys.

Detachable keypad

If you've got an Ericsson phone, you can fit a Chatboard. This is a small QWERTY keyboard which attaches to the bottom of the phone and enables you to text directly into the phone. It's small and light and whilst the keys are not very large, it is possible to type quite quickly. If you don't want to send a text message, you can unclip the keypad and use the phone as normal.

Ericsson Chatboard

Smart Partner

The Siemens C35i phone has a partner in the form of an IC35 digital handset. The handset features a QWERTY keyboard and LCD screen, and is linked to the phone with a cable. The data in both phone and keypad can be synchronised and the keypad can be used to enter text messages.

Purpose-built texter

An alternative approach to easing text entry is Motorola's V100. This phone looks like no other phone – more like a small personal organiser with its 'clam shell' design.

   With the optional earpiece you can use it as a phone, but its QWERTY keyboard makes it especially good for entering text messages. The keys are quite small, but it is much easier to text on this than on a phone. The trouble is, if you want to talk, it's not quite as easy to use as a conventional phone.

Personal Digital Assistants

Many modern Personal Digital Assistants (or PDAs) can be used in conjuction with a phone to send and receive text messages as well as managing other features like your phone's address book. If you have a PDA you'll first need to link it to the phone. If both your phone and your PDA have infrared capabilities then you're almost there. If you can't use infrared then you'll have to buy a cable which will have been specifically designed to link your particular PDA to your particular phone.

Motorola V100

WATCH
OUT

Cables to link your phone to a PDA can be
expensive.

If you need to buy a cable, first contact your PDA supplier. If you can't get one there, contact your phone supplier. There are several Internet sites that could help, but don't forget there aren't cables available to connect every PDA to every phone so it might not be possible to connect up your phone. The best solution (and the cheapest) is infrared.

Phone software to install on your PDA is available on the web, but once again there isn't software for every PDA and phone combination. Visit *http://www.tucows.com/* for a range of telephony software for most PDAs.

A Nokia 6110 connected to a Palm III organiser via an OPTION GSM adapter. With this setup you can send and receive emails as well as SMS messages. Text messages can be written on the PDA using the handwriting recognition software.

Which PDA should I buy?

The short answer to that is 'none', if all you want to do is find an easy way of entering text on your phone. They are just too expensive to be used solely for that purpose.

There are currently two types of PDA available – those with a keyboard and those without. Those that don't have a keyboard have a touch sensitive panel on the display in which you write. Yes, you actually write on the screen and the PDA translates what you've written into typed characters. The Palm Pilot was the first of this type and that led to later versions by Palm like the Palm V.

More recently Microsoft have developed the Pocket PC which is made by companies like Casio and Hewlett Packard. Keyboards are also absent from these and so text is handwritten

A Palm V personal digital assistant weighs less than most mobile phones and so can be carried around easily. It connects to your PC to enable all your messages to be saved. There are a variety of adaptors including one to connect to mobile phones.

onto the screen and character recognition software is used to translate what you've written into typed characters.

Handspring also make similar products based on the Palm Pilot operating system.

There are two types of PDA with a keyboard. The first manufacturer to make such a device was Psion. The latest models are the Series 5 and the Revo. Both have large keyboards which you can type on with ease (unlike some other QWERTY keyboards that are very small making typing difficult). Companies like Hewlett Packard and Compaq also produce PDAs with keyboards which run Microsoft software. Again, these are excellent products and most will connect to a variety of mobile phones.

COOL
TIP

If you're thinking about buying a PDA, it's worth considering whether it will connect to your phone.

LEARN BY
HEART

PDAs can do lots of computer tasks but are too expensive just for typing text messages.

The Psion Series 5 is one of several palmtop computers that can connect to a mobile phone for text messaging. Its keyboard is much smaller than a full size computer but is still very easy to use. Because it has an infrared eye, it can be connected to several infrared-capable phones without the need for a cable.

When sending a text message using your PDA, the phone and PDA must be linked (either by a cable or infrared) and when the two are 'talking to each other', you can begin. You enter the message on your PDA and when you send it the message goes from the PDA to the phone and then out of the phone just as it would if you'd entered and sent the message from your phone.

Graphics

You can send pictures with your text messages. Some phones include a small collection of pictures which you can attach to your message.

Although your phone might be able to send pictures, other people will not be able to read them if their phone doesn't support pictures.

Some Nokia phones have several pictures stored in them, and you can attach any one to a test message.

If it's a friend's birthday, send them a picture greeting.

Options

Text art

A variation on sending clipart images is to use text art. Bolt Blue (*http://www.boltblue.com/*) offer this service for free. They have an online list of images made up from characters like (.<*@%^,>/). The characters have been carefully put together and form a picture.

You have to register with Bolt Blue, which is free, and when your registration has been accepted you are sent a special code to your phone. When you log into the site, you must enter your name, password and the special code.

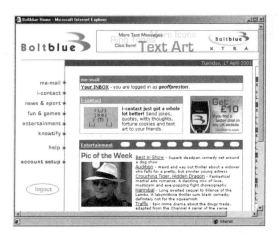

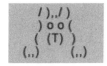

Variations

Sending a text message from a land line

You can send a simple text message to any mobile phone from a normal telephone line. Dial 07785 490 490 and you'll be connected to an automated answer service welcoming you to Vodafone Respond.

You can send to any mobile phone regardless of whether it's Vodafone, BT Cellnet, One2One, Orange or Virgin.

You'll first be asked to enter the number of the mobile phone you're trying to contact. Next enter the number of the phone you want the person to contact you on. Next enter a number for the message you want to send...

1. Please call {contact number} urgently

2. Please call {contact number} when convenient

3. Please call {contact number} today

4. Please call {contact number} tomorrow

Finally, press 0 to send.

This is an easy way for Mum and Dad to call you in.

Sending a Text Message from a Computer

You can send an SMS from your PC to a Vodafone mobile using HyperTerminal, which comes with Windows 98 and ME.

I   Load HyperTerminal and create a New Connection.

2   Enter the name for your new connection eg Vodafone.

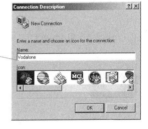

3   When you're asked to enter a phone number, enter 0385 499 998.

You may need to configure your modem, so click on Modify and then Configure. The settings should be...

Data Bits :	8
Stop Bits :	1
Parity :	None
Speed :	9600 bps

4 Click on **Connect**.

This is to send a text message to Vodafone only.

When you're connected, a message will appear...

You can send a maximum of two messages using this system. If you want to send more, you must log on again.

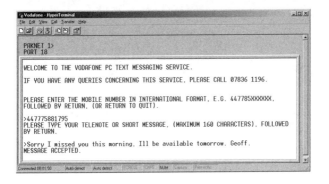

```
PAKNET 1>
PORT 18

WELCOME TO THE VODAFONE PC TEXT MESSAGING SERVICE.

IF YOU HAVE ANY QUERIES CONCERNING THIS SERVICE, PLEASE CALL 07836 1196.


PLEASE ENTER THE MOBILE NUMBER IN INTERNATIONAL FORMAT, E.G. 447785XXXXXX,
FOLLOWED BY RETURN, (OR RETURN TO QUIT).

>447775881795
PLEASE TYPE YOUR TELENOTE OR SHORT MESSAGE, (MAXIMUM 160 CHARACTERS), FOLLOWED
BY RETURN.

>Sorry I missed you this morning, Ill be available tomorrow. Geoff.
MESSAGE ACCEPTED.
```

5 Enter the phone number of the person you're trying to
   contact in international format, eg 447785xxxxx.

6 Write the message on your PC and press **Return** to send.

The message is then sent to the Text Message Centre and a
confirmation will be sent back to you if it has been accepted.

From the Web

Several websites offer text messaging. Lycos was one of the first
to offer this service and, at the time of writing, the service is
free. Once you're logged onto the Internet, go to
http://www.lycos.co.uk/service/sms/.

Find it, share it with Lycos

With Lycos you can send text messages from any computer in the world to any UK mobile phone. Its **free of charge** and you can send as many messages as you like.

Anyone with a digital mobile phone can now send and receive short text messages. It's the ideal way to keep in contact when you can't make or receive voice calls.

1 Click on the button marked **Send a message** at the bottom of the page.

2 Confirm that you agree with the terms of use.

3 Enter the mobile phone number of the person you want to send the message to, type in your message, and press Send.

Using software on your PC

There are programs readily available for you to install on your PC that will allow you to send text messages to mobile phones and, in some cases, to pagers. PageMail is one such program which can be downloaded from *http://www.dialogue.co.uk/*. (The download is on the Support page.)

Once installed, PageMail gives you a window into which messages can be typed directly from your computer's keyboard.

LEARN BY
HEART

The character limit still applies, but the current total is displayed just below your message.

Once a message has been typed, select the person you want to send it to, and click on the Send button. If you wish, you can send the message to more than one person at a time.

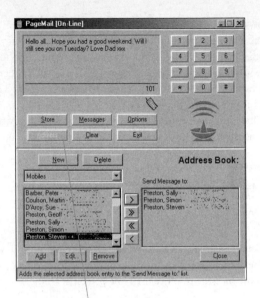

Clicking on the **Address** button opens a window containing the names and mobile phone numbers of your contacts.

Setup

Of course, as with all programs of this type, before you can use it, you need to spend a little bit of time setting it up.

You'll need to enter some information about your phone and your computer's modem. You can also enter a standard signature which will be added to the bottom of every message you send.

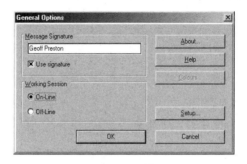

Email

If you're interested in sending emails from your mobile phone, or receiving emails on your mobile phone, check out the mobile email applications available from...

    Airmail   http://www.airmail.co.uk/

    BulletIN   http://www.bulletINmail.com/

If you haven't got a PC

Not everyone has a PC but even if you haven't you can still send text to a mobile phone.

The Amstrad E-Mailer is the first of a new generation of phones for use in the home. Where it differs from other home phones is that it has a QWERTY keyboard for entering text. It's marketed primarily as a device for sending emails, but what a lot of people don't know is that it can also send SMS messages.

The E-Mailer comes with its own pocket address pad which docks into the main console.

SMS Fax

A little-known fact is that if you can send text messages, you may be able to use the same equipment to send faxes. Vodafone's Telenote Fax is a system whereby users may create a text message on their mobile phone, but before sending it, prefix the recipient's fax number with 9741 in order to send it as a fax.

In an attempt to overcome the 160-character restriction imposed by SMS, Vodafone have thoughtfully included some short codes which are prefixed with an asterisk. When the fax is transmitted, the codes are translated into full sentences. There are currently 17 codes:

*10	CONFIRMATION
*11	URGENT
*12	FOR YOUR INFORMATION
*20	I will post the requested information today.
*21	Thank you.
*22	Please call me on my mobile
*23	Please call me at the office
*24	Meeting Cancelled
*25	Please call me at home
*26	I am on my way.
*27	Have a good weekend.
*28	See you later
*29	when convenient.
*30	urgently.

*31	I look forward to speaking to you soon.
*32	Meet me at
*33	Thank you for your time at our meeting. I look forward to speaking to you again soon.

You may also send a header containing subject, recipient and sender by using a hash (#)...

##Subject#Recipient#Sender#

To compose a Vodafone Telenote Fax, type in the message as normal, using the codes as appropriate. When sending, prefix the recipient's fax number with 9741 and send as normal. Shortly you'll receive an SMS message confirming successful transmission.

The following message translates into the fax on the opposite page, which contains over 300 characters. How many characters in the original message? The answer is on page 116.

##Sleepover#Maria#Sally#Do U want 2 sleepover 2nite? Mum & Dad R out. We can C a video 2gether. *25 this afternoon or *22 L8R. Sally

vodafone
FAX MESSAGING

To: Maria

Fax Number: █████████

From: Sally

Sender's Number: █████████

Subject: Sleepover

Date: 05/04/2001   Time: 12:16:37

Message Follows

Do U want 2 sleepover 2nite? Mum & Dad R out. We can C a video 2gether. Please
call me at home this afternoon or Please call me on my mobile L8R. Sally.

Message Ends.

vodafone - FAX AT YOUR FINGERTIPS

Chat

Some phones allow you to hold an SMS chat. To set up a chat,
you select Chat and enter your name (or nickname) and the
number of the person to whom you wish to chat. Type in your

message and send it. When the other person receives it, your name will be at the start of the conversation. To reply, the other person enters his/her name and your number. Then they enter a reply and send it.

In the example below, Alex sent a message to Sally. When the message arrived on Sally's phone it began with Alex:. Sally then replies and when it arrives on Alex's phone, the message begins with Sally:.

Both parties can see all of the conversation developing on the screen.

```
>Alex:Meet me
at the gates in
5 mins
<Sally:YEH
         OK
```

```
<Sally:YEH
THAT WILL BE
GR8. SEE U
L8R
         OK
```

COOL
TIP

This is a great way to have a chat without others
overhearing.

Receiving Text

When someone sends you a text message you'll know because
your phone will beep and a warning will appear on your phone
saying Message received. An icon (usually an envelope) will
appear on the screen indicating you have messages in your
phone that you haven't read.

If you've received just one message, most phones will allow
you to go directly to the message. If you've got more than one

Envelope icon

message, you'll probably have to go to your Inbox to view them. To get to your Inbox, open the menus, go to Messages and choose Inbox.

Managing messages

With a read message on the screen, you have several options available to you. If you really think you don't need the message anymore, you can Erase it.

COOL
TIP

Only erase messages that you really don't need anymore.

There is a limit to the number of old messages you can store in your phone, so you may need to erase old ones to make room for new ones.

If you can connect your phone to your PDA, use the PDA to store old text messages.

COOL
TIP

Many phones provide the opportunity to reply to a message you've received. Choosing this option means you don't have to enter the person's number. Once you've written your reply, it's simply sent back to the place that the message originally came from.

You can also forward a message you received to someone else. If you choose Forward, all you'll need to do is enter the number of the person you want to send it to.

A message sent to you may be intended for you only. Think before sharing it with others.

WATCH
OUT

Some phones have a built-in calendar. It's usually possible to copy a received message directly into a particular date on your calendar. If you can do this, there will be a menu option saying something like Copy to cal(endar).

Extracting numbers

If a friend wants to give you a phone number, you'll need to either memorise it as it's being given to you, write it down or try entering it into the phone as it's being given to you. Each method is less than satisfactory. Not many of us would be able to memorise an 11-digit number, and writing it down is fine if you happen to have a pencil, paper and something to rest the paper on as you scribble away. If you're at your desk writing it down may be possible, but if you're out in the street, taking out a notepad is not usually very practical. You can enter the number as it's spoken to you but you'll need to use a hands-free kit so you can see the keypad and listen to the message.

A clever and useful feature is the ability to extract telephone numbers that you receive as a text message.

When you receive a phone number in a text message...

Select **Options** and choose **Use number**.

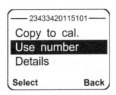

All of the groups of numbers that may be telephone numbers will be listed on the screen.

Any groups of numbers that could be a telephone number will be displayed, as is the case here where the message also includes a special code sent with the message.

2   Simply choose the number you wish to use and press either **Use** or **Call**, depending on which phone you're using.

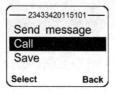

If you don't want to use the number immediately, you can leave it in the text message or save it into your phone's phone book for use later.

Directory enquiries

The logical extension of this facility is when you specifically request a number. Some service providers offer this feature, but currently not all. Directory enquiries' number is 192 and calling this on, say, Vodafone connects you to an operator in the same way as calling it on any phone – even a BT land line. The difference is that when the number you request has been found, it is sent as a text message to your phone. You don't need to request the number to be sent as a text message, it's done automatically and the name of the person or company you requested is included with the message.

```
┌──── 23433420115101 ────┐
│                         │
│  Vodafone               │
│  Directory              │
│  Assistance             │
│                         │
│  Options          Back  │
└─────────────────────────┘
```

Information alerts and other services

There are several companies who can send regular text messages
to your phone to provide anything from the latest world news
headlines, astrological forecasts, sports results and even the
National Lottery numbers.

My bank, for example, automatically send me a message
each week to tell me how much I've got, but also texts me if my
balance falls below a certain amount. Clearly the information
sent to me is different from that sent to other customers
because all the different bank accounts will hold different
amounts of money. But there are companies who will send
identical messages in bulk to lots of people.

WATCH
OUT

Some of these services are free, but there is a
charge for some.

Halebop: http://www.halebop.com/

You can arrange to have news and weather, horoscopes and stock quotes sent to your mobile phone for free.

Daily Quotes:
http://www.worldsms.com/

This service will send a quote each day in either English, German or Italian.

COOL
TIP

This could be a useful service if you're studying German or Italian.

eSMS.com: http://www.esms.com/

This website offers various SMS services including group SMS managing.

Vizzavi: http://www.vizzavi.co.uk/

Vodafone's Vizzavi service can send you the latest news, weather, horoscopes, sporting news, even lottery results. The service is free at present, but there may be a charge in the future. With a limit of 160 characters, the news is going to be very brief indeed – usually it's the headlines from three or four of the top stories. Similarly with the weather, don't expect a detailed long-range forecast for the entire country.

You have to register with Vizzavi but you can do it either online or by using your phone.

Give Us the Score:
http://www.giveusthescore.com/

This is a must for football fans. For less than 13p per week you can get the scores for your favourite team. For slightly more, you can get other information about each match including bookings.

Get the latest scores from Give Us the Score

My Alert: http://www.myalert.com/

Once you've registered, you can request all sorts of message alerts including sports results, horoscopes, pop news and National Lottery results. Share news is also available.

The service is free at present and includes the facility for sending a text message from your computer to a mobile phone.

Gozing: http://www.gozing.com/

You can earn rewards for text messaging that you can redeem at stores and websites.

MobileCrier: http://www.mobilecrier.com/

This free service sends text messages based on your specific interests, including news, travel, health, entertainment and business.

PageIQ: http://www.pageiq.com/

This website will send news headlines, weather reports and even traffic reports to your pager or phone.

Unified Messaging: http://www.unified-messaging.com/

This site offers email, fax, voicemail and SMS all in one inbox.

Watch My Server:
http://www.watchmyserver.com/registration/
index.php3

This service will send a text message to your mobile if your
server goes down.

COOL
TIP

You can even get computer virus alerts sent to
your phone.

Upoc Groups:
http://www.upoc.com/login.jsp

Upoc stands for Universal Point of Contact and provides you
with a friendly SMS mailing list of groups such as Celebrities.

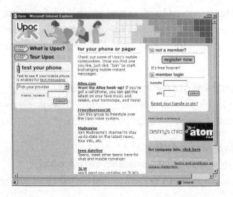

3

Graphics
for your Phone

At present there are two types of graphic that can be stored in your phone – Operator Logo and Group Graphics.

Operator Logo

When you switch on your phone and it receives a signal, it will display the name of the operator. In the UK this will probably be Vodafone, BT Cellnet, One2One or Orange. If you wish you can change this notice to a logo, hence it's known as an Operator Logo. It's intended to be the place where the operator can put their logo and do a bit of free advertising.

This is a GR8 way to personalise your phone.

COOL
TIP

The Operator Logo can be changed for something more personal to you. You'll see lots of adverts in daily newspapers offering them for immediate download to your phone. The list is endless. There are graphics of your favourite football team, star sign or favourite car. You can even have the logo of your favourite brand of training shoe!

Apart from phoning for a new logo, you can order one from the Internet where there are countless websites for you to choose a logo which will be sent directly to your phone.

The system is much the same for all companies offering graphics for your phone.

Using a telephone to order a graphic

1   Dial the number to get through to an automated message
    system.

2   Enter your mobile number.

3   Enter the code for the graphic you want.

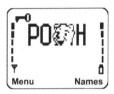

4   The graphic will arrive on your phone as a text message.

WATCH
OUT

You must ensure your phone is capable of
receiving the graphic. You will be charged even
if you cannot use the logo you have received.

Ordering a graphic from the web

1   Go to the website.

2   Register, or log on if you have previously registered.
(Registration involves entering your name and mobile
number, and perhaps a few other details like your service
provider.)

3   Enter the code for the graphic you want.

4   The graphic will arrive on your phone as a text message.

WATCH
OUT

Most sites charge for sending graphics, although
some are free. Try out the free ones first.

Some of the many companies offering this service are listed
on pages 135–143.

When you receive an Operator Logo, a message will be
displayed on your phone telling you. You can view the logo and
then decide whether to save it or discard it. If you choose to save

it, the new logo will replace any other Operator Logo you may already have saved.

WATCH
OUT

Most phones can only store one Operator Logo. Downloading another logo will delete one previously stored.

Some of the hundreds of Operator logos available

Group Graphics

All of the contact names in your phone's address book can be placed into Groups. Several groups are already defined, but their names can be changed. Those already defined include…

- Family

- Friends

- VIP

- Colleagues

Each group is given an icon (a small picture) which is displayed when a person from that particular group calls. The icon is called a Group Graphic and can be changed from the standard one supplied with the phone for another of your own design in much the same way as an Operator Logo. Companies who offer Operator Logos are gradually adding Group Graphics to their catalogue of images.

LEARN BY HEART

Do it Yourself

Downloading a new logo is fun, but more fun can be had designing an Operator Logo or Group Graphic yourself. There are websites where you can do it online (in which case they will send it into your phone for you), or you can download software and run it without going onto the Internet (in which case you'll need to connect your phone to your computer).

Downloading software

There are several programs available to design your graphics and move them into your phone. Kessler Design *(http://www.kessler-design.com)* have two programs...

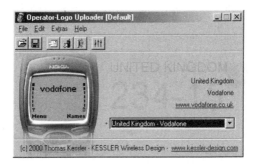

Operator-Logo Uploader. Use this program to choose an Operator Logo and upload it to your phone.

Group-Graphic Editor. Use this program to design and upload a Group Graphic and to design Operator Logos.

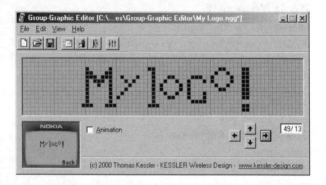

Both programs can be downloaded and used for a limited period of time, free. If you wish to keep one or both, you must register and pay a small fee.

COOL
TIP

Before buying either of these programs, ensure they work with your phone.

To use these programs you'll need to connect your phone to your computer. If your phone and your PC have infrared capabilities, then you have everything you need. If not, you'll have to buy a lead to connect them. First, check with your mobile phone supplier who should be able to help.

Setup

Both programs need to be set up before use. The setup procedure is the same for both programs.With the phone connected to your computer either via a cable or infrared, run the program in the normal way and...

1   Click on the setup button on the toolbar.

2   Ensure that the cable is connected to the correct port on your computer, or that you've selected infrared.

3 Enter the number of your mobile phone message centre in international format. Check page 33 for the correct numbers.

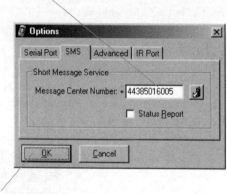

4 Click **OK**.

Operator-Logo Uploader

If you buy this program, it will come with several logos ready to upload. You can also log onto the Kessler Design website and download more for free.

To upload an Operator Logo...

| Connect your phone to your computer and run the Operator-Logo Uploader program.

2   Locate the logo you wish to upload.

3   Drag the required logo into the program window.

4   Select your service operator.

5   Click on **Send** icon.

6   Enter the number of the phone you wish the logo to be sent to...

7   ...and press **Send**.

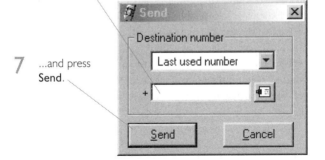

Group-Graphic Editor

Kessler Design's Group Graphic Editor is used for designing and editing Group Graphics and Operator Logos. It is also used to upload Group Graphics to your phone.

When the program has been downloaded from the Internet, installed in your computer and run, you get a window containing an enlarged representation of the area of your phone's screen where the icon is displayed.

Each of the squares represents a pixel (the smallest dot your phone's screen can display) and these can be switched on and off by clicking on them with your mouse. At the bottom of the window is a representation of the phone's screen approximately full size to show you what your new icon will look like on your phone.

Design area   Shift design up/down/left/right

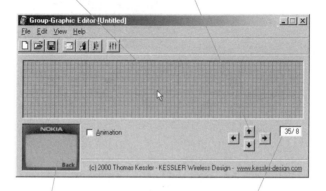

Representation of full size phone screen   Position of mouse pointer

Once you have designed your Operator Logo or Group Graphic...

Save it so that you can call it up later and alter it if required.

2 Click the **Send** icon.

3 Enter the number of the phone you wish to send the graphic to.

4 Click **Send**.

Both Operator Logos and Group Graphics will normally take less than a minute to reach your phone. When they arrive, you'll get a message warning you that either an Operator Logo or a Group Graphic has been sent to your phone. View the graphic first before deciding whether to keep it or discard it.

You can try as many as you like, but each upload will cost you the price of an SMS message.

LEARN BY
HEART

Designing Online

The disadvantage of the previous method of designing Operator Logos is that you need a means of connecting your phone to your computer. If you have infrared on both phone and computer, you're lucky. If not you've got to buy a cable specifically for your particular phone. The cables are quite expensive and if you later change your phone, the chances are the cable won't be compatible with your new phone.

Crazy Mobile offers online design which means you don't need a cable. To access the Crazy Mobile website, go to *http://www.crazymobile.co.uk/*. When the introductory screen appears choose either html or Flash site (the Flash site gives you more graphics and sound effects). Once you're into the site, choose Logo Painter.

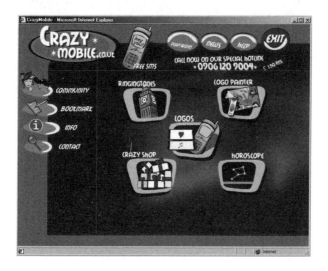

The main part of the design screen is a large scale representation of the area for the Operator Logo. There are a few pre-defined shapes you can use, or you can start with a blank screen.

When you've designed your logo, click on SEND, enter your mobile phone number and in about a minute, your logo will arrive in your phone.

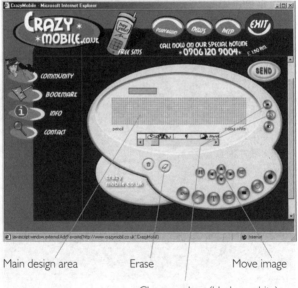

Main design area   Erase   Move image

Change colour (black or white)

4

Ringtones

Modern phones are really small but quite sophisticated computers, and like all computers, the decreasing cost of processing and computer memory has meant that phones have got cheaper. Many cellphones are now fitted with more processing power than they need to carry out the primary functions of a phone, ie to make and receive voice calls. As a result, the phone manufacturers have been trying to devise new and interesting features to make use of the surplus power and make the phones more attractive.

COOL
TIP

The traditional Brrr-Brrr, Brrr-Brrr ringing signal can now be replaced with any tune you like.

One of the most popular features are ringtones. Many phones are programmed with several tunes which can be played to alert you when someone is trying to call you. A more recent development is the ability to add to your phone's existing repertoire with ringtones that can be sent to your phone.

Ringtones can be sent to a mobile phone and selected to be played when someone tries to call you. As with graphics, ringtones can be ordered either from a phone or from the Internet.

LEARN BY
HEART

There is usually a charge for ringtones.

They are sent as a text message and when a new tone arrives in your phone, you'll have the chance to hear it first. If you like it, you can keep it, or if not, discard it.

WATCH OUT

There is a limit to the number of tones your phone can carry. If you have reached the limit, a new tone will delete one of the previously saved tones.

Once the ringtone has been received and saved, it must be selected from the list of ringtones.

COOL TIP

Phones which offer the user different Profiles can have different ringtones for different situations. Eg one tune for general use, another if you're outside and want a loud tune, another if you're inside and want a quiet tune etc. Some phones allow different ringtones for different caller groups so you can have one ringtone for friends, another for family etc.

A list of companies offering ringtones and graphics may be found on pages 135–143.

Jippii: http://www.jippii.co.uk/

To use this service you need to find a newspaper or magazine advert that lists the available tunes or graphics. You then send a text message to Jippii on 8501.

WATCH OUT

You really need to find the advert for the full catalogue or look at their website. Do not send a request for a tune or logo unless you've actually seen it advertised.

Begin the message with the word Tune or Logo (depending on which you want) and follow this with the name of the tune or logo from the list on the advert.

WATCH
OUT

This service will only work on a Vodafone network.

You can also order ringtones from the **jippii** website. If you don't like any of the tunes listed, you can now create your own ringtone online.

Do it Yourself

If you want something really personal, you can always write your own.

Using software on your PC

There are a few programs which will allow you to compose your own tune and send it to your phone. Nokring is one of the easiest to use but, as the name implies, is really for Nokia phones, although it may work with some of the other phones which are capable of receiving ringtones in RTTTL format. Check your phone's user manual to find out if it is compatible.

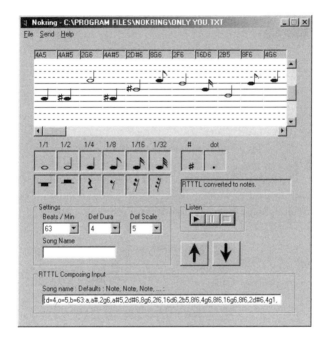

Nokring can be downloaded from the Internet by going to *http://www.cellular.co.za/nokring/intro.htm*. Once Nokring has been downloaded and installed, tunes can be entered, saved, loaded and edited on your PC. To send the tune to your phone, you'll need a cable to connect your phone to your PC.

The program is easy enough to use: simply drag notes onto the stave. Once you've created a tune, save it on your computer so you can edit it later.

With your phone connected to your computer, click on the **Send** button.

A window will open. Enter the mobile phone number you wish to send the tune to, and click the **Upload** button. The ringtone should arrive within about a minute.

Other Ringtone Software

Ringtone Converter:
http://www.bigfoot.com/jedmunds

If you have a Nokia 3210 phone you can enter ringtones on the
phone's keypad. This program converts the popular RTTTL
files into the format required for typing tones directly into a
3210.

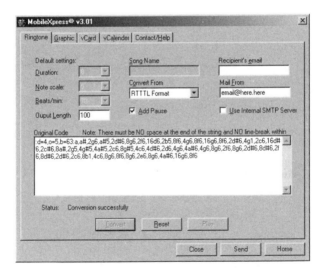

Mobile Xpress:
http://www.mobilesmarts.com/
download.shtml

This software converts popular ringtone formats such as RTTTL used by most Nokia phones to TDMA format. You can also contribute your own ringtones to a database of tones.

Answers

Page 2:   Hull is the only place to find telephone boxes painted cream.

Page 36:   There are 184 characters in the tip (including the text in brackets).

Page 78:   The original message contains just 132 characters.

5

WAP

The Wireless Application Protocol is a means of viewing Internet pages from a portable device thus enabling web surfing in the middle of a field or half way up a mountain. At present, the term 'WAP device' almost always means a WAP mobile phone and there are an ever-increasing number of them available.

DID YOU
KNOW

By 2004, over a third of all Europeans (220 million people) will access the Internet via a WAP-enabled phone.

As with all consumer electronics, the prices of WAP phones are falling. Not only the cost of the phones themselves, but the cost of accessing the Internet from a WAP device should gradually fall during the next year or two.

Before you can access WAP pages (or 'cards' to give them their correct title), you'll need a WAP phone.

Setup

To configure the phone to access the web you'll need an Internet Service Provider who has a WAP Gateway. (I use Demon, but there are plenty of others.) A quick phone call to your ISP will confirm if they do support WAP. If you've passed that stage, there are several options that need to be set on your phone. Clearly all phones are slightly different, although they will all have similar setup options.

Currently one of the most popular WAP phones is the Nokia 7110. If you go to the **Services** menu of a 7110 you'll find there are 11 options that need to be set...

7110 Setup

Homepage	This will begin *http://* and must be a WAPsite, not a website.
Connection type	Probably *Continuous*, but check with your ISP.
Security	Probably *Off*, but check with your ISP.
Bearer	*Data.*
Dial-up number	Your ISP's dial-up number which may be different to your usual dial-up number.
IP Address	You'll need to get this from your ISP – it will be four groups of up to three digits separated by full stops, eg *194.159.175.37.*
Authentication	*Normal.*
Data call type	*Analogue.*
Data call speed	This will probably be *Autobauding* but check with your ISP.
Username	The case sensitive name of your account .
Password	The case sensitive password (which must be entered twice).

COOL
TIP

At present, the Nokia 7110 is the most popular WAP phone in the UK.

What You Get

At 35 mm wide and 30 mm high, the Nokia 7110 has about the largest screen of any mobile phone, but even so the amount of WAP information displayed is limited. Graphics are virtually non-existent and the resolution pre-dates home computers of the late 1970s.

Like websites, the information available on WAPsites varies enormously in both quality and content but the most useful sites are those containing information or services that people are likely to need 'on-the-move'. Services such as weather reports, financial information and news feature heavily, but there are also numerous shopping sites selling such things as flowers and chocolates.

Technology being what it is, this market is set to expand and countless more examples of useful WAPsites will come online to add to the 4000+ UK WAPsites already up and running.

If you've succeeded in accessing the WAP, try visiting my WAPsite at *http://www.word4word.uk.com/wap.wml* where there is a special message for **in easy steps** readers.

Simulations

If you want to experiment with WAP, but don't have a WAP phone, there is an alternative, which is also a lot cheaper.

PyWeb: http://www.pyweb.com/

Visit **PyWeb**, download their WAP simulator, and view WAP on your desktop computer.

Gelon: http://gelon.net/

Gelon offers you a choice of nine WAP phones, and entering the address of a WAPsite is easier than using a phone as it's all done on the computer's QWERTY keyboard. Gelon freely admit that the simulations are not 100% perfect and probably never will be, because it's almost impossible to accurately translate WML (the WAP language) into HTML (the web language). That said, I couldn't find any bugs: holding my phone alongside the simulation showed that there wasn't much difference.

TagTag: http://tagtag.com/

There's an excellent WAP browser on the TagTag website which enables you to view WAPsites from within your web browser (eg Internet Explorer, Netscape etc). It's not based on any real-world WAP phone, but it does give a good approximation of what might be seen on phones in general, rather than one in particular.

WAPsites

The number of WAPsites is increasing rapidly. Here are some of the most popular…

LCI Technology	http://wap.lcigroup.com/
WAP Planet	http://www.wapplanet.net/wap/
WAP 0	http://wap0.com/
Mobile Invest	http://www.mobile-invest.co.uk/
moneyeXtra	http://wap.moneyextra.com/

BBC News	http://www.bbc.co.uk/mobile/mainmenu.wml
CitiKey	http://wap.citikey.com/
Flowerwap	http://www.flowerwap.co.uk/
Interactive Investor	http://mobile.iii.co.uk/
Newsvendor	http://wap.newsvendor.com/i.wml
Unmissable TV	http://www.unmissabletv.com/txw/wap.wml
Vizzavi	http://wap.vizzavi.co.uk/

WATCH OUT

Using a WAP phone is the most expensive way to access the Internet.

6

Phone Book Management

As computer processing has become cheaper, manufacturers of mobile phones have been able to add more and more features, whilst still keeping the price within the bounds of most people's budgets.

It didn't take long for the makers to include a phone book where you could store your regularly used phone numbers. This feature, which enabled you to easily contact friends without typing in their phone number each time you wanted to talk or text them, developed into an address book which could hold lots of other information about them, including, in some cases, email addresses and alternative phone numbers.

The introduction of a calendar meant that you could also include special dates and this in turn led to many phones being

LEARN BY HEART

Most modern phones have some form of organisational facility.

capable of performing functions normally associated with personal organisers.

The main drawback with a phone that thinks it's an organiser is the keyboard, or rather the lack of it. Just as text messaging suffers from a keypad that was originally designed to enter numbers, controlling the phone's on-board organiser features is quite tricky with only 10 or 12 keys on your phone's keypad.

If you have a cable to connect your mobile phone to your computer it might be worth getting a phone book management program that will enable you to do much of this work on your computer.

COOL TIP

If you change your phone, this is the best way to get all of the information from your old phone into your new one.

FoneSync

Nokia's FoneSync is one of several programs that will run on your PC and enable you to edit and update both your address book and your diary.

FoneSync can be downloaded from Nokia's website and installs on your PC in the usual way. When you have installed FoneSync, a shortcut is placed on the desktop and on the taskbar.

Running the program

First ensure the phone is connected to the computer and that you know which of the computer's ports it is connected to. This program supports infrared, so if your phone and computer can both communicate via infrared, this is the best way to do it. If you're using a cable, it will be attached to one of the computer's serial ports usually labelled Com1, Com2 etc. When installing software which involves connecting something to your computer, you'll sometimes be asked which port you are using although most software detects which port the phone is connected to.

When you have a connection, you will be told the computer and phone are communicating with each other.

When FoneSync is run for the first time, the Synchronization Setup screen will be displayed. Synchronisation enables you to get the details held in your phone into your computer, and the details held in your computer into the phone.

Clicking the **Synchronization Setup** button opens a window which gives you the option of synchronising your phone, the SIM card in your phone, or both. If you have more than one phone, you can choose which you want to work with.

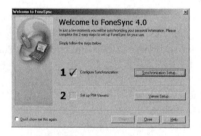

When you've decided what you want to do, click the **Next** button, tell the software whether you are using a cable or infrared and click on the **Finish** button.

You can perform a phone/computer synchronisation in two ways...

Click on the  button.

OR

Click the right mouse button over the FoneSync icon on the toolbar to open a menu.

From the menu, choose Synchronize.

This is the quickest way of updating the information held in the phone and in the computer as you don't have to run the the main part of the program.

When the synchronisation process begins you'll have the option of choosing whether to update the phone with information from the computer, or update the computer with information from the phone.

COOL
TIP

This should always be the first step – synchronise the phone and the computer to ensure you're starting with common data.

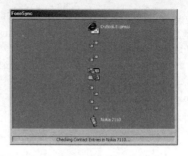

When you begin synchronising, a graphic shows the data flowing between your phone and the computer.

You can also decide whether to synchronise the phone book, the calendar or both. You can also choose which other software you want to synchronise with, eg Microsoft Outlook.

All of the functions you can do on your phone, you can do using FoneSync, but with FoneSync it's much easier.

The main FoneSync window is divided into two parts. On the right is the work area (in this case, the phone book) and on the left is a panel from where you can choose which set of information to work with. You can edit all of the information from the phone as well as being able to add new names, contact details and events. The phone book window allows you to enter lots of different information about contacts.

COOL TIP

Use a synchronisation program to keep the details saved in your phone safe in case you lose it.

It's worth getting phone management software for entering contact details, but if you want to use your phone as an organiser and you intend entering dates for parties, exams or concerts, this type of software is essential.

LEARN BY HEART

Losing your phone is bad enough, but it can be replaced fairly easily. If you lose all the information within the phone it may not be so easy to replace.

Using your phone to enter notes is quite tricky, partly because of the very limited amount of information that can be displayed on the phone's screen. You'll have to make several selections from a variety of menus which includes choosing the date you want to make the note for, and the type of note you want to enter.

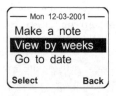

Using FoneSync

I   Click on the date you want from the calendar at the top right of the window.

2   Double-click on the time of the day, and a new window opens into which you can add an event.

The details can then be entered, including whether or not you want the phone to warn you when an event is close.

FoneSync is a free download and there is a version for several different Nokia phones. You can download the software from *http://www.nokia.com*

Alternatives

FoneSync is but one PC application which helps you manage your phone's contact list and events diary, but there are others.

SIMsuite by Fone Range:
http://mobilefun.co.uk

Mobile Fun supply a huge range of products for mobile phones including data cables, infrared eyes and software to enable you to edit your phone's address book and calendar.

PhoneFile by Pipistrel:
http://www.pipistrel.com/phonefile

PhoneFile Lite is free software, without time limits or use restrictions. It's a cut-down version of PhoneFile Pro (which you have to pay for) but still has lots of features. With the Lite version you can edit and transfer your SIM phone book entries. It works with any GSM-compatible SIM but you will need a SIM reader which connects to your PC.

7

Numbers
and Websites

This chapter contains some of the many phone-related websites and phone numbers.

Tones and Graphics

Acme Tones
0906 633 0100/2
http://www.acmetones.co.uk/
Tones for Nokia, Sagem and Motorola, Graphics for Nokia.

Bolt Blue
http://www.boltblue.co.uk/

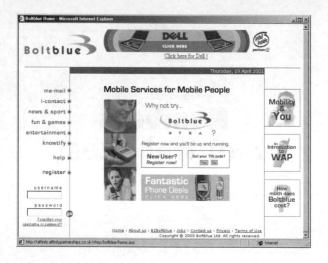

Carphone Warehouse

0800 424 800

http://www.carphonewarehouse.com/

Tones and Graphics for Nokia.

Crazy Mobile

0906 120 9006/6817/9

http://www.crazymobile.co.uk/

Tones for Nokia, Sagem and Motorola, Graphics for Nokia.

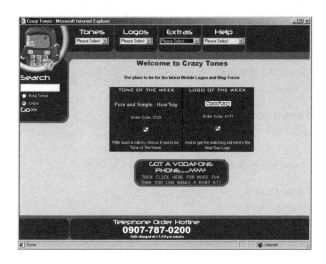

Crazy Tones

0907 787 0200

http://www.crazytones.co.uk/

Tones and Graphics for Nokia and Sagem.

Dial a Logo

0906 120 9018

http://www.dialalogo.co.uk/

Tones and Graphics for Nokia.

Findatone

0907 787 0220/1

http://www.findatone.co.uk/

Tones for Nokia and Sagem, Graphics for Nokia. Tones for Ericsson and Siemens from website only.

Fonedream

0906 400 2212

http://www.fonedream.com/

Tones for Nokia and Sagem, Graphics for Nokia.

Fonetastic

0808 002 0200

http://www.itouch.co.uk/

or http://wap.itouch.co.uk/

Tones and Graphics for Nokia.

Funnyfones

0906 633 2740/2754/2001

http://www.funnyfones.com/

Tones and Graphics for Nokia.

Icon A Phone

0906 952 5299

http://www.iconaphone.com/

Tones for Nokia and Sagem, Graphics for Nokia.

Logo First

0906 633 0005/0080

http://www.logofirst.com/

Tones and Graphics for Nokia.

Logo Hell

0907 787 2800

http://www.logohell.co.uk/

Tones for Nokia, Sagem and Motorola, Graphics for Nokia.

Logo Paradise

0906 736 5301/0264

http://www.logoparadise.com/

Tones and Graphics for Nokia and Sagem.

Logos and Ringtones

0906 466 0298

Tones and Graphics for Nokia.

Loony Tones

0907 787 8383

http://www.loonytones.co.uk/

Tones and Graphics for Nokia.

Mobile Mania

0906 170 0069

http://www.tonemania.com/

Tones for Nokia, Sagem and Motorola, Graphics for Nokia.

Monster Mobile

0906 120 2313/6759

http://www.monstermob.com/

Tones and Graphics for Nokia.

Ringtone City

0906 120 6997/9076

http://www.ringtonecity.co.uk/

Tones and Graphics for Nokia and Sagem.

The Ringtone Factory

0906 636 8600

Tones and Graphics for Nokia.

Smileyfones

0906 633 1021

http://www.smileyfones.com/

Tones and Graphics for Nokia.

Tone Mania

0906 170 0024

http://www.tonemania.com/

Tones for Nokia, Sagem and Motorola, Graphics for Nokia.

Tones and Graphics

0906 400 8000

Tones for Nokia and Sagem, Graphics for Nokia.

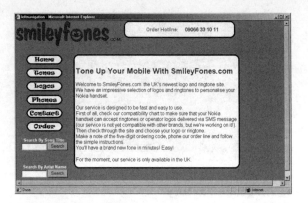

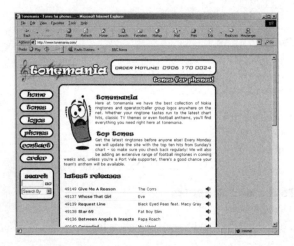

Unique Logos
0907 787 7712/2298
http://www.uniquelogos.co.uk/
Tones for Nokia, Sagem and Motorola, Graphics for Nokia.

Unique Tones
0907 787 2800
http://www.uniquetones.co.uk/
Tones for Nokia, Sagem and Motorola, Graphics for Nokia.

Service Providers
The five main UK service providers are...

0808 100 2392
http://www.btcellnet.net/

0500 500 121
http://www.one2one.co.uk/

0500 802080
http://www.orange.co.uk/
index.html

0845 6000 600
http://www.virgin.com/mobile

01295 815000
http://www.vodafone.co.uk/

COOL
TIP
Compare the different services carefully. All offer different phone costs and call costs. Check what your friends have. It's often cheaper to call Vodafone to Vodafone, One2One to One2One etc. Check cheap rate and local call costs.

Phone Manufacturers

Some of the main phone manufacturers are...

   http://www.ericsson.com/

   http://www.motorola.com/

   http://www.nokia.co.uk/

   http://www.philips.com/

   http://www.sagem.com/

SIEMENS   http://www.siemens.co.uk/

COOL
TIP

Before deciding on a particular phone, check the features. Are you paying for gimmicks you won't use, or are there features you really want? Look at the features described in this book and decide what might be important to you.

Retailers

These are the high street shops and mail order companies who sell phones either with or without a contract. Buying a phone with a contract results in a cheaper phone, but higher call costs.

Advanced Communications
0800 091 5151
http://www.advancedmobiles.co.uk/

Call4Phones
0800 054 6272

Carphone Warehouse
0800 424 800
http://www.carphonewarehouse.com/

Connect@fone
0800 018 4455

Club Mobile
0800 138 6628
http://www.clubmobile.co.uk/

THE **Carphone Warehouse**
COMMUNICATION CENTRES

Dial-a-Phone
0800 000 077
http://www.dialaphone.co.uk/

Digital Cellphones
0500 000 121

Direct Fone Warehouse
0800 043 0400

Don't Buy
0800 043 4504
http://www.dontbuy.co.uk/

DX Communications
0800 085 8858
http://www.dxcomms.co.uk/

e2save
0800 019 2219
http://www.e2save.com/

Free Fones Direct
0870 744 0027

First for Mobiles

0800 035 3310

kjc

0800 959 999

http://www.kjcmobile.com/

Mobile Fun

0121 355 2332

http://mobilefun.co.uk

Mobile Phone Centre

0800 200 100

http://www.mpc.co.uk/

Mobile Phone Store

0800 22 44 77

http://www.themobilephonestore.com

Odyssey Direct

0870 444 8881

http://www.ocp2000.com/

OneStopPhoneShop
0800 034 5557
http://www.onestopphoneshop.co.uk/

Phones4U
0800 096 4490
http://www.phones4udirect.com/

The Pocket Phone Shop
01753 214 421
http://www.pocketphone.co.uk/

The Link
0500 222 666
http://www.thelink.co.uk/

Virgin
0845 6000 810
http://www.virgin.com/

Vodafone
0800 10 11 12
http://www.vodafone-retail.co.uk/

Walk 'N' Talk
0800 043 1000

Index